I'm Going to Pet a Worm Today
and Other Poems

I'm Going to Pet a Worm Today
and Other Poems

By Constance Levy
Illustrated by Ronald Himler

Margaret K. McElderry Books
New York

Maxwell Macmillan Canada
Toronto

Maxwell Macmillan International Publishing Group
New York   Oxford   Singapore   Sydney

Margaret K. McElderry Books
Macmillan Publishing Company
866 Third Avenue
New York, NY 10022

Maxwell Macmillan Canada, Inc.
1200 Eglinton Avenue East
Suite 200
Don Mills, Ontario M3C 3N1

Printed in the United States of America
10 9 8 7 6 5 4 3 2

Library of Congress Cataloging-in-Publication Data
Levy, Constance.
I'm going to pet a worm today : and other poems / by Constance
Levy ; illustrated by Ronald Himler.
p.   cm.
Summary: Thirty-nine poems about everyday things, mostly nature,
from leaves on trees to eating peas and petting worms.
ISBN 0-689-50535-3
1. Children's poetry, American.   [1. Nature—Poetry.   2. American
poetry.]   I. Himler, Ronald, ill.   II. Title.
PS3562.E9256I16   1991   811'.54—dc20   91-7485

"Tree Coming Up," © 1975 by Constance Levy, first appeared in the March
1975 issue of Cricket.

"I'm Going to Pet a Worm Today," © 1975 by Constance Levy, originally entitled "I'll Tell Emily,"
first appeared in the April 1975 issue of Cricket.

"Snow Feet," © 1991 by Constance Levy, first appeared in the January 1991 issue of Cricket.

To Monty,
our children, and grandchildren

and remembering with love
my parents, Samuel and Esther Kling
—C.L.

Contents

TREE COMING UP

A shoot, a shoot,
A greenish boot
Kicks open the door
Of the acorn house.
A split, a crack, a baby oak
Begins to push and stretch and poke
By a worm at home in a tunnel bed,
Past ants at work,
Past beetle nooks,
Through earth as rich as brown nut-bread
Tree coming up—look out ahead!

OUT

I like *out*
better than *in*
but *in* is where
my days begin;
in is for sleeping
and waking up
and bathtubs and such,
but I don't like *in*
nearly as much
as toes in the dew
and the mist on my face
and the sky for my roof—
my favorite place
is *out*: out where
the world is showing.
I don't care if a
storm is blowing.
Step aside *in* because I am going
out!

DAWN WATCH

The sky divides itself
in two:
West is velvet
dark and blue,
sleepy stars
still peeking through.

East is lemony and light
and all the stars
have slipped from sight.
      I stretch one arm
       to meet the day
the other reaches
back to night.

MORNING GRASS

In shadow light
out walking early
to see the grass
refreshed with pearly dew,
I, too,

would be a blade
the sky has touched—
awakened to a world still hushed,
wind whispering,
my face dew-washed . . .

THE COLOR-EATER

Sunset mixed this recipe:
Orange and grape and raspberry,
Folded in and spread between
Lemonade and nectarine.
Too, too tempting
Don't you think
All that orange and
All that pink,
All that purple,
All that yellow?
Who could blame
The hungry fellow?
Night came sniffing
Like a pup;
Licked it
Liked it
Lapped it up!

GREEN THINGS

I'll name some green things:
Let me see . . .
a four-leaf clover
(lucky me!),
dancing grass
when spring rain falls,
a slick cucumber's
overalls . . .
the green the summer oak tree wears
to camouflage
a squirrel's stairs;
an artichoke, a lime, the sea,
a fresh bouquet of
broccoli,
and somewhere in a forest hollow
a slim green snake
too quick to follow.
   Now, time for lunch.
   What will it be?
   Why, all the pea soup
   we can swallow!

BIG AND LITTLE

From a tiny little chip
in the middle of a step
where a thimbleful of water
from the sprinkler collects,
a very thirsty robin
who was watching from the lawn
has come to take a little sip;
and as I walk along
I think of all the big things:
the sky, the lawn, the tree,
and a little robin waiting for
an opportunity . . .

I'm Going to Pet a Worm Today

I'm going to pet a worm today.
I'm going to pet a worm. Don't say,
"Don't pet a worm"—I'm doing it soon.
Emily's coming this afternoon!
And you know what she'll probably say:
"I touched a mouse," or
"I held a snake," or
"I felt a dead bird's wing."
And she'll turn to me with a kind of smile.
"What did you do that's interesting?"
This time
I am
Going to say,
"Why, Emily, you should have seen me
Pet a worm today!"
And I'll tell her he shrank and he stretched like elastic,
And I got a chill and it felt fantastic.
And I'll watch her smile
Fade away when she
Wishes, that moment,
That she could be me!

Encounter on a Yellow Flower

Nose, don't breathe—
so near your tip
a butterfly dares
to take a sip;
so close, I fear
she'll hear me think;
so bold her eyes,
mine must not blink!

Lips, don't speak—
I see her draw
the liquid through
her slender straw.
She pulls so hard
she seems to frown;
her cheeks fill up,
she gulps it down.
But you, heart,
thumping like a drum
will scare her off
before she's done!

QUESTIONS TO ASK A BUTTERFLY

When you're out
and round about
what comes first:
fun or thirst?
Do you count the time
by flowers?
How many hours
in your day?
How do you play?

Do the purple ones
taste yummy?
How many sips
will fill your tummy?
How do you land with
so light a touch?
Do you ever eat too much?
Why won't you stay?

LIMERICKS

How awkward while playing with glue
To suddenly find out that you
Have stuck nice and tight
Your left hand to your right
In a permanent how-do-you-do!

***

An anteater noses the ground,
He walks that way all through the town.
If you say, "My, how queer!"
He will perk up his ear
And reply, "That's where most ants are found!"

But Only the Breeze . . .

I found the robin lying still
beside the shed.
Its orange side was down,
its wings half spread.

I wanted it to flutter, rise
up to the sky;
I begged it to try . . .

But only the breeze
that lifted a wing,
only the breeze,
did anything.

CONNECTION

One blade
of slim green grass
beside another;
between them a silver thread
where a spider
has tied them
together.

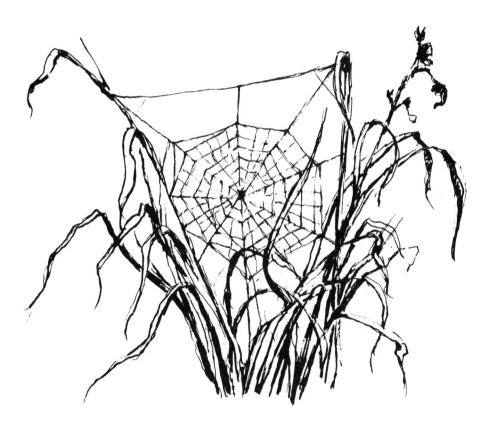

THE BUSINESS OF BEES

Bees, bees, bees,
the clovers are sizzling with bees
they're dizzy with bees
they're terribly busy with bees,
and the bees are a-buzz
with the business of bees.
And that's how it is
and that's how it was
before you and I
even were us . . .

THE KISS

A once-upon-a-butterfly
is on my hand; his kiss
is lighter than a petal falls—
I think he is a prince

enchanted when, in once-upon-a-
time, a wicked witch
transformed him; now he wants
another chance to be a prince.

I draw him gently closer as he
clasps his wings above him
and hopes that I'm the one at last
to really, truly love him.

I am—I *was*!
He would have been
a prince by now. I miss him.
He flew away just as I bent
my face to his
to kiss him.

GREEN BEETLE

A little green beetle—
he does not stir
as I walk around him
like a customer,
looking,
stopping
to admire
the way he glows
with emerald fire.

Have you ever met
a beetle like that?
But shhhhhh. He's asleep
on a pillow of sun
and I'd rather not wake him
just yet.

ENOUGH IS ENOUGH

This little brown ant
found a blue jay's feather.
He is trying to do
what he can't—he will never
carry that feather away.

His mandible clamps on the barbs
like a lion to attack,
and he digs in his toes for the pull,
but the feather fights back!

Now he pushes . . . no luck,
it has stuck on a bump
in the walk.
Still he doesn't give up.

He runs round the feather
and clamps a new spot,
and he's pulling with all
of the strength he has got,
but this feather is tough!

He lets go and runs off
through the dust;
even ants know
enough is enough!

THE COLLECTOR

We ants collect odd things, oh why
can't I resist? I always try
to be selective
and keep track
of what I have
and what I lack,
but then a seed
a bit of fluff
a crumb of some delicious stuff
an odd-shaped piece of bric-a-brac
calls out to me
to bring it back
and I,
no matter how I try,
can not say no.
I wonder why . . .

STRAY CAT

A cat becomes a habit
if you take
her offer of two golden eyes
like golden eggs.
A cat becomes a habit
you can't break.

And if you take the eyes
she gives you more:
a rubdown on your ankles
with her fur,
and she dangles
at your ears
a silver purr.

Make no mistake—
be careful what you take;
a cat becomes a habit
you can't shake!

THE GUYS AND I AND THE HUMMINGBIRD

We sat around and talked about the team
when like a fastball tearing through the air
a hummingbird zoomed right across our heads
and didn't seem to care that we were there.

He dipped his spikelike beak into a flower.
I saw a splash of red upon his throat;
the faintest little sound came from his wings
as if the air around him hummed a note.

He hung there like a bud without a stem;
then dipped again. I liked his shade of green.
Nobody spoke. Then quickly as he came
zoomed off before we swallowed what we'd seen.

THE GARDENER

Hoeing rows and sowing rows
that's the way a gardener goes;
my brother, James, is one of those.

Lifting soil and sifting soil
till it works with ease,
that's the work a gardener knows.
My brother, James, is planting peas.

Raking where you need to rake
breaking clumps of earth to make
airy beds for plants to grow
weeding, seeding till you ache!

That's what James does. Watch him take
much more time than you would think
planting every precious pea
extra-special carefully.

Even lunch will have to wait.
James says, "Just another minute
till I make this row run straight
with perfectly placed pea seeds in it!"

RAH, RAH PEAS!

Don't say,
"Awwww, peas!"
Try some
Raw peas!

New peas!
Sweet peas!
Great fresh
Treat—peas!

Zip the pods and
Pop 'em in
You won't stop
Once you begin!

You'll scream,
"More, Please!"
Rah! Rah!
Raw peas!

CARDINAL IN THE GARDEN

The lettuce, beans, and broccoli are host
to yellow butterflies. Upon a post,
resplendent as a red geranium,
the cardinal looks out. He seems to boast:
   Yes, color makes the bird
   and I am one
   who's just about as handsome
   as they come!

SLEEPY TIME

Caterpillar sleeps
in a silky locket
squirrel in a leafy popcorn ball
new kangaroo takes his nap in a pocket
mud dauber wasp in a jug on the wall.

Hippopotamus sleeps
on his pals in a puddle
quail tail to tail
in a turned-around huddle
cat all wrapped up with herself in a ball
and earthworms and bees like to snuggle and cuddle

but
bats
hang
on racks
by their socks
for their naps!

WEEDS

Whenever you're around weeds:
    the brittle stalks of brown weeds
    the burly purple ball weeds
    the lanky seed-topped tall weeds

    the scraggy shaggy rag weeds
    the seeds-inside-a-bag weeds
    the rods of flowered gold weeds
    the thistly, prickly bold weeds

the trick is knowing which weeds
are scratchy, make-you-itch weeds
and which of these are sneeze weeds!

Meadow Walk

The field mice dart like minnows
away from where we walk,
and underneath in shadows
some secret crickets talk.
We wade through waves of grasses
and seeds and weeds and bees,
and try to keep the spider silks
from sticking to our knees.

BIRDSEED SONG

We split the seeds
We pick the pits
We poke about for favorites;
We look around between each pick
And fidget while we're doing it

It's corn we nip in little chunks
It's bits and chips of oats and wheat
It's tasty tips of toasty weeds
And millet, milo, sunflower seeds

It's chunks
   and chips
      and bits
         and tips
And millet, milo, sunflower seeds!

Where Have the Beetles Gone?

Where are all the crickets
that were singing in the hedges
and the ants enjoying crumbs we left
from lunches on the benches
and the spiders on the bridal wreath
embroidering their fences?
Oh, it's really rather lonely
on a cold and empty lawn
when you're used to having beetles.
Where have all the beetles gone?

September Butterfly

It was time to go
but she had a few
last-minute things
she had to do

like sharing a rose
with a sleepy bee
and resting a while
on the hawthorn tree

and dancing around
like a day in July
kissing chrysanthemums
one last good-bye.

CROW TREE

I do not know those crows,
I did not hear one say,
"Hey, guys, I'm really beat,
let's park our feet, okay?
Let's have a show of wings
from everyone who thinks
we should spread out on this tree
and all grab forty winks."

But I *do* know I find
they make a great design
and I hope the crow that said it
gets the credit!

THE OLD LEAVES

The old leaves
try to sleep
on the grass
but the breeze
says, "Sleep?
How boring!"

So it blows on their noses
    and tickles their toes
        till they
toss
    turn
        wiggle and twitch
scratch at an itch
fidget and switch
from that side to this
restless as fish.
    Listen—
        now they're snoring!

WINDSTORM

Something
of major proportions
is loose in the air.
Something
grabbed hold of the roof
and is trying to shake it.
The branches are doing contortions
and tearing their hair.
That bully!
We want it to stop
but no one can make it.
So hold tight
to your hat
when you're out—
or that something will take it!

SNOW FEET

Step
Break the crust
Sink in white dust
Repeat

Your legs
Lift
Chunks of concrete

A snow walk's a slow walk
When snow drifts are deep

Step
Break the crust
Sink in white dust
Repeat—
Like breaking in
Two
Brand-new
White feet.

WHAT WATER WISHES

Water looks thin
but weighs thick.
Pick up a bucketful—
it pulls you back;
sings you its wild
ocean songs
as it sloshes, swishes,
trying to say,
Take me back to where water belongs!
That's what all water wishes.

A HOUSE

Oh, the wonderful sound
of the pounding of nails
the wheeze of the sawblades
the buzzes and squeals
the struts and the joists
and the hoist of the beams
the sandbanks of sawdust
the levels and planes
and the strong sweet foresty
breath of the wood
like a mist—
as a piece of a place
that was only a space
is becoming a house!

THE STORY OF RUBBER BALL

Rubber ball
sat all alone.
A caterpillar
crawled by it,
pulling himself.
A spider
tried it
and decided
it was the wrong size.
A bumblebee buzzed it.
An ant missed it
by a millimeter.
A woodpecker
picked at it,
poked at it,
pecked at it,
and pocked it all up.
Rubber ball
sat all alone
till a Labrador retriever,
lolling along,
tucked it into
his tight white teeth
and took it home
to keep.

DRAWING DUCKS

I'm really good at drawing ducks
I make them very yellow
I always make them following
the leader in a row
I always make them walking left—
and then I wonder *where they go*!

I give each one an orange bill
Each eye I dot just so . . .
and then they look at me so hard
it makes me wonder
what they know!

MENU

Liverwurst on pumpernickel,
whole wheat toast, or white;
mustard, lettuce, and a pickle;
frosty orange delight;
hamburger on bun, a slice of
cheddar, Swiss, or mozzarella;
taco chips or fried potatoes;
Lox on bagel;
sliced tomatoes . . .

"I will take your order,"
says the waiter to us snackers.
(We are very busy eating
all the little wrapped-up crackers.)
Then he neatly pours the water
but the table is a mess
with the crumbs and cracker wrappers
which he cleans up, more or less

and we order—all the same
for it's hamburgers again
which we *knew* before we came.

A GOOD NIGHT

With a blanket new or a blanket frayed
a quilt that somebody's great-aunt made
a cover that's light
or soft and white
or knitted, crocheted—
any kind is all right

if you cover me warm
and tuck me tight
and "love me in"
with a kiss good night.